Return to Real Love

By

Travis Suarez-Taylor

Copyright

About the Author

Travis Suarez-Taylor is the author of Return to Real Love, a reflective work focused on healing, emotional clarity, and intentional connection.

Dedication

This book is dedicated to anyone who has ever felt emotionally misunderstood, unheard, or unsure how to express what they were feeling.
To those who have loved deeply, lost themselves along the way, questioned their worth, or stayed too long in situations that no longer aligned—this is for you.
May these pages serve as a mirror, a pause, and a reminder that clarity is possible, healing is intentional, and real love begins within.

ACKNOWLEDGEMENT

This book was born during a season of reflection, healing, and awakening. It exists because of the quiet moments, the hard conversations, the unanswered questions, and the growth that followed.

I want to acknowledge every experience that shaped this journey—the lessons that challenged me, the moments that humbled me, and the clarity that came from choosing alignment over comfort. To those who crossed my path during times of confusion, growth, and self-discovery, thank you. Each interaction played a role in revealing deeper truths about love, boundaries, and emotional responsibility.

I am grateful for the people who encouraged honesty, self-awareness, and healing, whether they knew they were doing so or not. This book reflects learning how to listen inward, trust the process, and return to what is real.

Most importantly, I acknowledge the courage it takes to pause, reflect, and choose growth. This work is for anyone willing to look within and begin again with Intention.

Table of Contents

Chapter 1: Awakening

I used to believe love was supposed to hurt a little. Not in the obvious, dramatic ways people warn you about, but in quieter ways that they felt normal because they were familiar. Tension. Uncertainty. Emotional heights followed by long stretches of confusion. For a long time, I thought that was just part of loving deeply.

What I didn't realize back then was how much of my understanding of love came from survival, not safety.

When you grow up learning how to adapt, to read moods, to anticipate reactions, to keep peace—you can confuse emotional effort with emotional connection. You learn how to show up, how to give, how to stay. What you don't always learn is how to be held without performing.

So I kept choosing love that required me to prove myself.

I told myself I was patient. Understanding. Loyal. And I was. But underneath those qualities was a pattern I hadn't named yet: I was overextending in places where I should have been observing. I was giving before I was grounded. I was committing myself before I was secure.

The truth is, real love doesn't require you to abandon yourself.

That realization didn't come all at once. It came in fragments of exhaustion, quiet disappointment, the feeling of being emotionally present in spaces where I wasn't emotionally met. I would ask myself why I felt drained after connection, why closeness felt like work instead of rest.

For a long time, I ignored those questions.

It's easier to stay busy than to be honest. Easier to blame timing, circumstances, or "bad luck" than to admit you're repeating a cycle you learned a long time ago. But cycles don't break themselves. They repeat until you pause long enough to see them clearly.

Awakening, for me, wasn't about blame. It was about awareness.

I began to understand that love rooted in chaos feels exciting because it mirrors instability we already know. Calm can feel unfamiliar, even boring, when your nervous system is used to intensity. But unfamiliarity doesn't mean wrong. Sometimes it means healthier.

Real love started to look less like emotional fireworks and more like emotional safety.

Safety doesn't announce itself loudly. It shows up in consistency. In conversations that don't leave you questioning where you stand. In effort that feels mutual instead of measured. In moments where you don't have to shrink, perform, or explain your worth.

As I started paying attention to how my body felt in different connections, I noticed something important: peace felt different than relief. Relief came after tension. Peace existed without it.

That distinction changed everything.

Awakening wasn't about becoming someone new. It was about returning to myself, before I learned to equate love with endurance. Before I believed that being chosen meant being depleted.

Real love, I realized, begins when you stop abandoning yourself to be accepted.

And once you see that clearly, there's no going back.

End of Chapter 1

Chapter 1 Reflection

What does real love mean to me today?
 What patterns am I leaving behind?

Chapter 2: Seeing the Red Flags

Red flags are rarely invisible. More often, they're uncomfortable. Subtle. Easy to explain away if you're invested enough in the outcome.

I didn't miss red flags because I couldn't see them. I missed them because I didn't want to interrupt the story I was hoping would unfold.

When you want something to work, you can turn almost anything into a temporary issue. Inconsistency becomes "they're busy." Emotional distance becomes "they've been through a lot." Lack of accountability becomes "no one's perfect." You start editing reality to protect potential.

I did that more times than I want to admit.

At first, the signs felt small. Conversations that never went deeper than the surface. Effort that showed up inconsistently. Moments where I felt like I was leaning in while the other person stayed comfortably back. None of it felt alarming on its own. But patterns don't reveal themselves in single moments; they reveal themselves over time.

And time always tells the truth.

There's a quiet voice inside those notices when something feels off. It's the pause after a text that doesn't sit right. The tightness in your chest when plans fall through again. The feeling of being emotionally available while someone else remains selectively present. I heard that voice, but I didn't always listen.

I told myself I was being patient. Understanding. Flexible.

What I was really being was accommodating at my own expense.

Ignoring red flags isn't about being naïve. It's about being hopeful. Hope can be a beautiful thing, but when it's not grounded in reality, it becomes a way of bypassing your own boundaries. You stay because you believe things will change, even when nothing is changing.

The lesson didn't come from one relationship ending. It came from recognizing the same emotional dynamic showing up in different faces. Different names. Different timelines. Same feeling.

That's when I had to ask myself a harder question:
Why am I attracted to what feels familiar instead of what feels secure?

Red flags aren't always about danger. Sometimes they're simply information. They're indicators of misalignment, differences in readiness, emotional capacity, or intention. The problem isn't noticing them. The problem is negotiating with them.

I learned that clarity doesn't come from confrontation alone. It comes from observation. From allowing people to show you who they are without filling in the gaps for them. From paying attention to actions, not potential.

What I learned most was this:
If something consistently makes you feel uncertain, unseen, or unsettled, that feeling is already an answer.

You don't need proof to honor your intuition. You don't need permission to step back. And you don't need to wait for things to get worse before you choose differently.

Seeing red flags isn't about judgment. It's about self-respect.

Once I stopped explaining away what didn't feel right, I created space for something that did.

And that's when my standards stopped being theoretical and started being lived.

End of Chapter 2

Chapter 2 Reflection

When have I ignored red flags?

What did I learn from that experience?

Chapter 3: Emotional Safety

I didn't always know how to name emotional safety. I just knew when it was missing.

There's a difference between being close to someone and feeling safe with them. Closeness can happen quickly. Safety takes time. It shows up not in grand gestures, but in the way, conversations are held, in how conflict is handled, in whether your honesty is met with curiosity or defensiveness.

For a long time, I thought chemistry was enough. If the connection felt strong, I assumed safety would follow. But chemistry without safety creates confusion. You feel drawn in, yet constantly on edge. Present, but guarded. Interested, but unsure.

That tension lives in the body before it ever reaches the mind.

I started paying attention to how I felt during and after interactions. Did I feel settled or stimulated? Relaxed or alert? Did I feel like I could be fully myself, or was I choosing my words carefully to avoid misunderstanding, conflict, or withdrawal?

Those questions told me more than words ever could.

Emotional safety doesn't mean the absence of disagreement. It means knowing that disagreement won't cost you connection. It means being able to express discomfort without fear of punishment. It means your feelings aren't minimized, rushed, or used against you later.

In unsafe dynamics, vulnerability feels risky. You share something real, and it's met with silence, deflection, or a shift in energy. Over time, you learn to hold back. To filter. To protect yourself. And slowly, intimacy erodes, not because you stopped caring, but because you stopped feeling safe enough to show up fully.

I didn't realize how much I was bracing in certain connections until I experienced the opposite.

Emotional safety feels like exhaling. Like being understood without having to overexplain. Like consistency between words and actions. Like knowing where you stand without needing constant reassurance.

It's subtle, but it's unmistakable once you know it.

I also learned that emotional safety is mutual. It's not just about how someone treats you, it's about how you show up for them. Are you listening to understand, or listening to respond? Are you present, or distracted? Are you open to repair or committed to being right?

Safe connection requires responsibility on both sides.

One of the biggest shifts for me was realizing that anxiety in a connection wasn't a sign of passion, it was a signal. A signal that something needed attention, clarity, or honesty. Ignoring that signal didn't make it disappear. It only made it louder over time.

When emotional safety is present, love doesn't feel like something you have to manage. It feels steady. Grounded. Alive without being overwhelming.

That's when I understood something important:
Love that feels safe doesn't dull you, it frees you.

And once your body learns what safety feels like, it becomes much harder to accept anything less.

End of Chapter 3

Chapter 3 Reflection

What does emotional safety feel like in my body?

Who provides that consistently?

Chapter 4: The Cost of Overgiving

For a long time, I believed giving more would create security. If I showed up consistently, offered support freely, and made myself dependable, then connection would deepen naturally. Love, I thought, was something you earned through effort.

What I didn't understand then was the difference between generosity and self-erasure.

Overgiving doesn't start as a problem. It starts as care. As intention. As a genuine desire to show up for someone you value. But when giving becomes a way to secure attachment, to be needed, appreciated, or chosen, it slowly turns into a strategy rather than an expression.

I didn't always notice when the balance shifted.

I would say yes when I was tired. Offer understanding when I was hurt. Make space for someone else's emotions while quietly sidelining my own. On the surface, it looked like maturity. Inside, it felt like depletion.

Over time, resentment crept into not because I was giving, but because I wasn't being met.

The hardest part about over giving is how invisible it can be. People don't usually ask you to abandon yourself. They accept what you offer. And if you don't set limits, they have no reason to know where those limits should be.

I learned that boundaries aren't punishments. They're information.

Overgiving often comes from a fear of loss, the belief that if you stop giving, you'll stop being valued. That fear can be powerful, especially if you've learned early on that love requires effort to maintain. But love that disappears when you stop overextending isn't love rooted in mutuality.

Its love rooted in access.

There's a quiet moment when you realize you're doing more emotional labor than the other person. When you're carrying conversations, initiating repair, offering reassurance—while your own needs go unaddressed. That moment can be easy to ignore. But it's also a turning point.

For me, recognizing the cost of over giving meant asking a different question. Not "How can I do more?" but "What happens if I do less?"

What happens if I pause before responding?
What happens if I express discomfort instead of smoothing it over?
What happens if I let someone meet me where I am, instead of meeting them where they're comfortable?

The answers weren't always comfortable. Some connections have shifted. Some faded. But what remained felt more honest.

I learned that real connection doesn't require constant sacrifice. It requires presence, reciprocity, and respect. Giving from fullness feels different than giving from fear. One sustains you. The other slowly drains you.

Overgiving taught me an important lesson:
Love shouldn't cost you your sense of self.

When you stop pouring from an empty cup, you create space for connection that nourishes instead of consumes.

And that space is where balance begins.

Chapter 4 Reflection

Where do I overgive?

What am I afraid will happen if I stop?

Chapter 5: Boundaries as Self-Respect

For a long time, I thought boundaries were walls. Something rigid. Defensive. A sign that you were closing yourself off instead of leaning in. I associated them with distance, not care.

What I didn't understand was that boundaries aren't about pushing people away. They're about letting the right people stay.

Without boundaries, everything feels personal. Every shift in tone, every unmet expectation, every inconsistency becomes something you internalize. You start adjusting yourself to maintain connection, even when it costs you clarity or peace.

I did that more times than I can count.

Setting boundaries forced me to confront an uncomfortable truth: I was afraid of how people would respond if I was honest about my limits. I worried that saying no would make me difficult, unavailable, or unloving. So instead, I stayed agreeable, and quietly overwhelmed.

But boundaries don't require aggression. They require clarity.

A boundary is simply an agreement you make with yourself about what you will and won't accept. It's not about controlling someone else's behavior. It's about deciding how you respond when your needs aren't respected.

I learned that peace doesn't come from managing other people's expectations. It comes from honoring your own.

The first boundaries I set felt awkward. I stumbled over my words. I second-guessed myself. I wondered if I was being unfair or too sensitive. But over time, something shifted. I felt less resentful. Less depleted. More grounded.

And I noticed something else: the people who respected my boundaries didn't disappear. They adjusted.

Those who relied on my lack of boundaries, however, struggled. Some pushed back. Some minimized my feelings. Some slowly drifted away. That hurt, but it also revealed something important.

Boundaries don't change people. They reveal them.

Real love doesn't require you to overextend or stay silent. It makes room for honesty. It honors limits. It understands that two whole people choosing each other is healthier than two people losing themselves to stay connected.

I also learned that boundaries need consistency. You can't set a limit and then abandon it when it's inconvenient. Doing that teaches others, and yourself, that your needs are negotiable.

They're not.

Boundaries protect your energy, your time, and your emotional well-being. They create a foundation where trust can grow because expectations are clear. When you know where you stand, there's less room for confusion or resentment.

Setting boundaries didn't make me colder. It made me more intentional. More present. More available for connections that were grounded in respect rather than endurance.

Boundaries are not barriers to love.
They are proof that you value yourself enough to receive it fully.

End of Chapter 5

Chapter 5 Reflection

What boundaries protect my peace?
Where do I need to enforce them?

Chapter 6: Chaos Isn't Passion

For a long time, I confused intensity with depth. If something felt unpredictable, emotionally charged, or consuming, I told myself it meant the connection was strong. The heights felt euphoric, the lows felt dramatic, and somewhere in between, I called it passion.

What I didn't realize was how familiar chaos had become to me.

When your nervous system is used to inconsistency, calm can feel unsettling. Silence feels like distance. Stability feels like boredom. You start craving emotional spikes, not because they're healthy, but because they're recognizable.

I chased that feeling without questioning it.

The problem with chaos is that it keeps you focused on survival instead of connection. You're always reacting, trying to fix, soothe, reassure, or regain footing. There's little space to simply be present. Little room for curiosity, growth, or mutual understanding.

And yet, chaos can feel intoxicating at first. It creates urgency. Attachment. The illusion of closeness. But urgency is not intimacy, and volatility is not depth.

I noticed how exhausted I felt in relationships that were fueled by emotional swings. How often I was bracing myself, waiting for the next shift, the next misunderstanding, the next moment where I'd have to steady the ground again.

That kind of love doesn't nourish you. It drains you.

Calm intimacy, on the other hand, doesn't announce itself loudly. It unfolds steadily. It allows for rhythm instead of reaction. Conversations don't feel like landmines. Disagreements don't feel like threats. You're not constantly wondering where you stand.

At first, calm felt unfamiliar to me. Almost suspicious. I had to sit with the discomfort of not being emotionally activated all the time. I had to learn that peace didn't mean lack of interest meant security.

Calm intimacy shows up as reliability. Emotional availability. Presence without pressure. It's the feeling of being chosen without having to compete for attention or reassurance.

I also learned that chaos often disguises itself as chemistry when boundaries are weak. The emotional pull feels strong because there's uncertainty. But uncertainty isn't a prerequisite for desire, it's a warning sign.

When love is grounded, you don't need to decode it. You don't need to constantly check the temperature of the connection. You're not stuck in cycles of hope and disappointment.

Choosing calm required me to slow down. To listen to my body instead of chasing emotional adrenaline. To trust that steadiness could still hold excitement, depth, and joy.

And it can.

Chaos keeps your alert.
Calm allows you to rest.

Once I understood that difference, I stopped romanticizing what destabilized me—and started honoring what made me feel whole.

End of Chapter 6

Chapter 6 Reflection
Where have I confused chaos for passion?
What does calm intimacy look like?

Chapter 7: Attention vs. Intention

For a long time, I mistook attention for care. If someone showed interest, stayed in contact, or expressed desire, I assumed it meant they were invested. But attention and intention are not the same thing—and confusing them can keep you emotionally stuck.

Attention feels good in the moment. It validates. It reassures. It fills gaps when you're uncertain about where you stand. But intention is revealed over time. It shows up in consistency, follow-through, and aligned actions, not just words.

I had to learn that the hard way.

There were moments when I felt chosen because someone reached out often, shared pieces of their life, or made me feel seen in flashes. But when I stepped back and looked at the whole picture, something didn't add up. Plans stayed vague. Effort came and went. Conversations circled without moving forward.

I was receiving attention, but not direction.

Intention carries clarity. It doesn't leave you guessing. It doesn't rely on emotional breadcrumbs to maintain connection. When someone is intentional, their interest has momentum. There's movement, purpose, and accountability behind their actions.

I started asking myself different questions:
Do their words match their behavior?
Do they make space for me consistently, or only when it's convenient?
Do I feel grounded, or am I constantly waiting for reassurance?

Those questions cut through confusion quickly.

Attention without intention can feel intoxicating because it keeps hope alive without requiring commitment. It allows someone to enjoy connection without responsibility. And if you're not paying attention, you can end up investing deeply in something that was never meant to grow.

I realized that real interest doesn't require you to chase clarity. It offers it freely.

When intention is present, effort doesn't feel sporadic. Communication doesn't feel performative. You're not wondering if you're asking for too much simply by asking for consistency.

The shift for me was learning to pause instead of leaning in harder. To observe patterns instead of filling in gaps. To let someone's behavior tell me what their words couldn't.

I learned that it's okay to want more than attention. It's okay to desire direction, depth, and follow-through. Wanting intention doesn't make you demand, it makes you discern.

Attention can be flattering.
Intention is grounding.

Once I understood that difference, I stopped settling for connections that felt good temporarily but went nowhere. I made room for relationships that were moving with purpose, not just momentum.

And that made all the difference.

End of Chapter 7

Chapter 7 Reflection

Am I receiving love or attention?
What evidence supports that?

Chapter 8: The Conversations We Avoid

There's a moment in every connection where silence becomes a choice. Not because there's nothing to say, but because saying it feels risky. I learned that avoiding difficult conversations doesn't protect relationships. It slowly weakens them.

I used to tell myself I was choosing peace. That bringing things up might create tension, disrupt harmony, or push someone away. So instead of naming what felt off, I adjusted myself. I stayed quiet. I waited.

But unspoken truth doesn't disappear. It settles in the body. It shows up as distance, resentment, or emotional withdrawal. And eventually, it speaks anyway, just not in words.

The conversations we avoid are usually the ones that matter most.

I noticed that when I hesitated to speak honestly, it was often because I was afraid of the response. Afraid of being misunderstood. Afraid of being seen as too much. Afraid that clarity would reveal misalignment I wasn't ready to face.

Avoidance felt safer than knowing.

But safety built on silence isn't safe, it's delay.

Real intimacy requires courage. Not the loud kind, but the quiet willingness to be seen. To say, "These matters to me," even when you don't know how it will land. To ask questions that invite truth instead of maintaining comfort.

I learned that timing matters, but readiness matters more. Waiting for the "perfect moment" often meant waiting indefinitely. And in that waiting, connection stalled.

When conversations are avoided, assumptions fill the gap. You start interpreting tone instead of asking for clarity. You read between lines that were never written. And slowly, the relationship becomes more about managing uncertainty than building understanding.

Honest conversation doesn't guarantee alignment, but it reveals it.

Some truths brought us closer. Others showed me that we were standing in different places emotionally. Both outcomes were valuable. Both offered direction instead of confusion.

I also had to learn that how you communicate matters as much as what you say. Speaking from curiosity instead of accusation. Naming feelings instead of assigning blame. Creating space for response instead of control.

The goal of hard conversations isn't to win. It's to understand.

When truth is welcomed, trust grows. When it's avoided, distance does.

I stopped seeing difficult conversations as threats and started seeing them as invitations—to clarity, to honesty, to alignment. Not every connection survives that invitation. But the ones that do are stronger because of it.

Silence may feel easier in the moment.
But truth is what makes connection sustainable.

End of Chapter 8

Chapter 8 Reflection

What conversations am I avoiding?
What truth needs to be spoken?

Chapter 9: Raising the Standard

There comes a point where clarity turns into choice. Where knowing what you deserve isn't enough, you must decide whether you're willing to honor it.

For me, that moment came when I realized how often I tolerate things I said I didn't want. Not because I lacked standards, but because I didn't always enforce them. I knew what felt misaligned, yet I stayed. I hoped. I adjusted.

Standards don't matter if they aren't lived.

I used to think having standards meant being rigid or unrealistic. That wanting more would narrow my options or make me difficult to love. But the truth is, standards don't push away what's meant for you; they filter out what isn't.

Raising your standard isn't about demanding perfection. It's about consistency. Respect. Emotional availability. It's about choosing connections that meet you where you are instead of asking you to lower yourself to meet them.

I learned that tolerating behavior you don't accept teaches people how to treat you. Silence becomes permission. Staying becomes endorsement. And over time, the gap between what you say you want and what you accept grows wider.

That gap is where self-trust erodes.

Raising the standard required me to get honest with myself. To stop negotiating my needs. To stop explaining away patterns that didn't align with the kind of love I wanted to build.

It also required me to walk away sooner. Not angrily. Not dramatically. But clearly.

Walking away isn't failure. It's alignment.

I learned that when your standards are clear, you don't need ultimatums. You don't need to be convinced. You simply observe, decide, and respond accordingly.

High standards don't make you unapproachable. They make you intentional.

They signal that your time, energy, and emotional well-being matter. That you're not interested in potential without effort. That you're not building connections based on hope alone.

As I raised my standards, my circle became smaller, but healthier. Quieter, but more grounded. I stopped chasing validation and started choosing alignment.

And the most important standard I raised was this:
I would no longer stay where I had to convince myself to be okay.

That decision didn't make love harder to find.
It made it clearer.

End of Chapter 9

Chapter 9 Reflection

What behaviors will I no longer tolerate?
What standard am I honoring?

Chapter 10: Choosing Green Flags

For a long time, I was more fluent in what to avoid than in what to seek. I knew the red flags well. I could spot inconsistency, emotional unavailability, and mixed signals from a distance. But knowing what you don't want is only half the work. At some point, you must get clear about what you *do* want.

That's where green flags come in.

Green flags aren't dramatic. They don't rush you or overwhelm you. They're steady, often subtle indicators that something is healthy, aligned, and worth nurturing. And if you're not paying attention, they can be easy to overlook, especially if you're used to intensity being the measure of connection.

I had to retrain my attention.

I started noticing how it felt to interact with people who communicated clearly. Who followed through on what they said. Who showed interest without pressure. Who respected my boundaries without taking them personally.

Those qualities didn't create emotional spikes. They created trust.

Green flags show up as consistency. Emotional presence. Curiosity about who you are, not just how you make someone feel. They show up in the willingness to have honest conversations, to repair misunderstandings, to take responsibility without defensiveness.

They also show up in how someone treats themselves. Self-awareness. Accountability. A willingness to grow. These things matter because you don't just build a relationship with someone, you build it with the patterns they bring with them.

One of the biggest shifts for me was realizing that calm interest doesn't mean lack of attraction. It means emotional regulation. It means someone isn't trying to fast-track intimacy or avoid it altogether. They're allowing it to unfold naturally.

Choosing green flags requires patience. I had to resist the urge to fill silence with meaning or assume that slower pacing meant less interest. It often meant more intention.

I also learned that green flags feel grounding in the body. You're not anxious. You're not bracing. You're not asking where you stand. There's room to be yourself without strategizing how to be received.

That kind of connection doesn't always announce itself loudly, but it lasts.

By choosing green flags, I wasn't lowering my expectations. I was refining them. I stopped chasing emotional heights and started prioritizing emotional health. I stopped confusing familiarity with compatibility.

And once I knew what green flags looked like, I stopped overlooking them.

Because real love doesn't just avoid harm.
It actively supports growth, safety, and mutual respect.

End of Chapter 10

Chapter 10 Reflection

What are my top green flags?
What patterns am I choosing now?

Chapter 11: Lessons from Solitude

Solitude has a way of revealing what noise keeps hidden. When there's no one to impress, no dynamic to manage, no expectations to meet, you're left with yourself, and that can be uncomfortable at first.

For a long time, I treated being alone as something to move through quickly. A pause between connections. A temporary state to endure until the next relationship arrives. I didn't see it as a teacher. I saw it as absence.

That perspective shifted when I stopped filling the space.

Without distraction, patterns became clearer. I noticed how much of my identity had been shaped around showing up for others. How often do I prioritize connection over introspection. How rarely did I ask myself what *I* needed without filtering it through someone else's expectations.

Solitude created room for honesty.

In the quiet, I had to confront the parts of myself I used to overlook, the need for rest, the fear of stillness, the habit of measuring worth by usefulness. There was no one else to validate or distract from those realizations. Just awareness.

And that awareness was grounding.

I learned that being alone doesn't mean being incomplete. It means having the space to become more whole. To reflect without urgency. To heal without performance. To redefine what fulfillment looks like when it isn't mirrored back by another person.

Solitude taught me self-trust. When you make decisions without external validation, you learn to listen inwardly. You learn which impulses come from fear and which come from alignment. You learn that you can sit with uncertainty without rushing to resolve it.

It also showed me the importance of pacing. Of letting things unfold instead of forcing timelines. When you're comfortable alone, you're less likely to attach to potential out of fear of emptiness.

I began to appreciate my own presence. The quiet routines. The small moments of peace. The sense of stability that comes from knowing you can meet yourself with compassion instead of criticism.

Solitude wasn't something to escape anymore. It became something to protect.

Because the relationship you build with yourself sets the tone for every other relationship that follows.

When you learn how to be alone without feeling lonely, you stop choosing connection from a place of lack. You choose it from wholeness.

And that changes everything.

End of Chapter 11

Chapter 11 Reflection

What has solitude taught me?
How has healing changed me?

Chapter 12: Protecting Your Energy

There was a time when I believed being available was the same as being loving. If I responded quickly, stayed accessible, and made space for everyone else's needs, I thought I was doing the right thing. What I didn't understand was how easily availability can turn into depletion.

Energy is not unlimited. And how you spend it matters.

I began noticing how certain interactions left me feeling drained while others left me grounded. The difference wasn't always obvious at first. Sometimes it showed up as subtle fatigue. Other times such as irritability, restlessness, or a sense of being stretched too thin.

Protecting your energy doesn't mean withdrawing from connection. It means choosing where you invest intentionally.

I had to unlearn the idea that rest was something you earn after doing enough. Rest is not a reward, it's a requirement. When you ignore that, burnout follows quietly, often disguised as commitment or responsibility.

I started paying attention to my boundaries around time, communication, and emotional labor. I noticed when I was taking on other people's feelings without being asked. When I was problem-solving instead of listening. When I was staying engaged out of obligation rather than desire.

Those moments were signals, not failures.

Protecting your energy also means honoring your rhythms. Knowing when you need space. When you need connection. When you need silence. And allowing yourself to respond accordingly without guilt.

I learned that saying no doesn't close doors, it preserves capacity. It allows you to show up more fully where it matters most. It keeps resentment from building quietly in the background.

There's a difference between being supportive and being self-sacrificing. Support has limits. Sacrifice erodes them.

As I became more mindful of my energy, my relationships shifted. Some deepened. Others naturally faded. That wasn't loss, it was alignment. The connections that remained felt more reciprocal, more grounded, more respectful of the fact that presence is a choice, not an obligation.

Protecting your energy isn't selfish. It's responsible. It ensures that when you give, you're doing so from fullness, not exhaustion.

And when your energy is protected, your relationships have room to breathe.

End of Chapter 12

Chapter 12 Reflection

What choices am I making differently?
How am I protecting my energy?

Chapter 13: Trusting Timing

There was a season when I believed that if something was meant to happen, it would happen quickly. I equated urgency with alignment. If connection flowed easily, I assumed it was right. If it stalled, I questioned myself.

What I eventually learned was that timing isn't about speed. It's about readiness.

Trusting timing required me to slow down and listen differently. To stop forcing outcomes and start paying attention to what felt aligned in the present moment. Not what I wanted to rush toward, but what was unfolding naturally.

There's a difference between patience and postponement. Patience is grounded. It feels steady. Postponement feels heavy, like you're waiting for something to change without any real movement. Learning to tell the difference helped me stop lingering in spaces that weren't evolving.

Timing also revealed where I was trying to control outcomes instead of participating in them. When I pushed too hard, I often overlooked signals that something wasn't ready, whether that was a relationship, a conversation, or a version of myself that still needed growth.

Alignment doesn't require force.

Trusting timing meant honoring where I was emotionally. It meant recognizing when I was healed enough to show up fully, and when I still needed space to integrate lessons I'd already learned. Growth isn't linear, and rushing it only creates repetition.

I learned to ask better questions:
Does this feel calm or pressured?
Am I choosing this from clarity or from fear of missing out?
Does this add to my life as it is, or am I hoping it will change it?

Those questions grounded me in the present.

Trusting timing doesn't mean passivity. It means responsiveness. It means showing up when things feel aligned and stepping back when they don't. It means trusting that what's meant for you won't require you to abandon yourself to receive it.

Some things arrive later than expected but arrive healthier because of it.

When I stopped rushing love, I created space for it to meet me where I was, not where I thought I needed to be. And that made all the difference.

End of Chapter 13

Chapter 13 Reflection

Where am I being asked to trust timing?
What feels aligned right now?

Chapter 14: Love That Feels Safe

For a long time, I thought safety in love meant certainty, knowing where things were going, having clear labels, or feeling assured that nothing would go wrong. But real safety turned out to be something quieter and more embodied.

Love that feels safe doesn't keep you guessing.

It's the feeling of being able to show up as you are, without editing your emotions to be more acceptable. It's knowing that your honesty won't be punished, dismissed, or used against you later. Safety lives in how someone responds when things aren't perfect.

I noticed that when love felt unsafe, I was constantly monitoring myself. Choosing words carefully. Anticipating reactions. Managing emotions instead of expressing them. That kind of vigilance is exhausting, even when affection is present.

Safety removes that need.

When love feels safe, communication flows more naturally. You don't avoid difficult topics—you approach them with trust. Disagreements don't feel like threats. They feel like opportunities for understanding. Repair happens without defensiveness.

I learned that safety isn't the absence of conflict. It's the presence of respect during it.

Love that feels safe also honors autonomy. There's room for individuality without fear of distance. Space doesn't feel like abandonment. Togetherness doesn't feel like obligation. You can be close without losing yourself.

That balance is powerful.

I began to recognize safety in consistency. In reliability. In emotional presence that didn't waver based on mood or circumstance. In effort that felt mutual instead of transactional.

Safety showed up in the small moments: follow-through, listening without interruption, accountability without excuse. These weren't grand gestures—but they mattered more.

I also learned that safety starts within. When you trust yourself, you're less likely to tolerate dynamics that undermine your peace. You don't cling to uncertainty. You don't chase reassurance. You choose connections that reflect the stability you've cultivated internally.

Love that feels safe allows you to rest. To exhale. To grow without fear of losing connection.

And once you experience that kind of love, even briefly, you understand something clearly:

You never want to build with anything else.

End of Chapter 14

Chapter 14 Reflection

What makes love feel safe to me?
How do I show up authentically?

Chapter 15: Choosing Real Love

Real love doesn't arrive all at once. It's built, slowly, intentionally, through the choices you make when no one is watching. Through what you tolerate, what you release, and what you commit to honoring moving forward.

By the time I reached this point, my understanding of love had changed. Not because I'd found something perfect, but because I'd found clarity. I knew what felt aligned. I knew what didn't. And most importantly, I trusted myself enough to choose accordingly.

Real love isn't about intensity. It's about integrity.

It's the alignment between words and actions. The willingness to show up consistently, even when things feel ordinary. The ability to hold space for another person without losing yourself in the process.

I learned that love isn't proven through endurance. You don't have to suffer to show commitment. You don't have to shrink to stay connected. Love that requires you to abandon your values, silence your needs, or compromise your peace isn't love, it's attachment.

Choosing real love meant choosing myself first. Not in isolation, but in wholeness. It meant honoring the lessons learned from past patterns without carrying their weight forward. It meant releasing the need to repeat what was familiar to feel worthy.

Real love feels grounded. It feels mutual. It feels safe enough to grow in, not perform in.

I also learned that choosing real love doesn't guarantee certainty. It doesn't promise timelines or outcomes. But it does promise alignment. And alignment brings peace, even in the unknown.

There's courage in choosing differently. In walking away from what no longer serves you. In staying open without abandoning discernment. In trusting that the love meant for you will meet you where you are, not where you pretend to be.

As I moved forward, I committed to honoring what I'd learned:
• To listen to my intuition
• To uphold my boundaries
• To value consistency over chemistry
• To choose calm over chaos
• To prioritize emotional safety
• To remain open without self-betrayal

Real love isn't something you chase. It's something you allow by becoming aligned with it.

And when you do, love stops feeling like something you must survive.

It becomes something you get to share.

End of Chapter 15

Chapter 15 Reflection

What does real love look like moving forward?
What am I committed to honoring?

Travis Suarez-Taylor

Travis Suarez-Taylor writes about emotionally grounded, faith-centered relationships and personal alignment. His work focuses on clarity, emotional intelligence, and the courage to choose peace over chaos.

Through lived experience, reflection, and honest dialogue, Travis encourages readers to trust their intuition, recognize misalignment, and return to love rooted in truth, consistency, and emotional safety.

www.ingramcontent.com/pod-product-compliance
Lightning Source LLC
Chambersburg PA
CBHW022013170726
47994CB00026B/3181